T0164976

SOARING WITH EAGLES

REVELING IN SUNNY SPACES
&
DIVING INTO GORGES

Devotional Meditations Upon
The Book Of James

By James Gibson

ISBN: 978-1-4269-7444-1 (sc)
ISBN: 978-1-4269-7445-8 (e)

Trafford rev. 09/19/2011

 www.trafford.com

North America & international
toll-free: 1 888 232 4444 (USA & Canada)
phone: 250 383 6864 ♦ fax: 812 355 4082

TABLE OF CONTENTS

DEDICATION

To the memory of K Blair
Who demonstrated for so many of us
the reality that we could be grateful for sufferings
and thank God for them.

PREFACE

I kept a journal of my daily meditations for years. They were based upon scripture, as are these in *Soaring With Eagles*. Ultimately, they were shared with more than 60 subscribers over the Internet. Positive responses prompted me to write the book hoping that you and others might benefit from it.

I have recorded my prayers as a conclusion to each devotional meditation. Most of these prayers include a response that I perceive coming from God. I hope this will not be misinterpreted as trying to speak for God. Those responses are my honest interpretation of how God responds to me. I am fully aware that I am capable of misunderstanding God. But, I strongly believe that prayer should include time for listening to God.

I have recently shared these meditations with a men's Bible study that meets each Sunday morning at a local restaurant. Their responses have also encouraged me to undertake writing the lessons from James into publishable form. James is not an easy book to study, but it is one of my favorites because it never fails to challenge me to become a better person. It is my hope that readers of this book will join me in wanting to become better persons. Receptive spirits are the key to becoming better persons, for God can take open, hungry hearts and make something beautiful of them.

James Gibson
May 1, 2011
Bangs, Texas

INTRODUCTION

James, Jesus' half brother, has left us a treasure. He has instructed us in the way to live a Christian life. He tells us how to deal with suffering better than any other biblical author. He speaks to many, for there are many who have experienced and who are experiencing suffering. When friends ask, "How can I tell if I am going to experience suffering?" I answer, "Place three fingers upon your forehead, and if you are warm, then you will experience suffering."

James tells us that we are to be happy when suffering comes upon us. The line waiting to speak with James in Heaven is going to be a long one. I hope to be in that line, for I want to recite my heartbreaks and ask, "Did you intend that I be happy about this?" I already anticipate James' answer, "Yes!" Suffering stretches us and awakens the character that God has already placed within us. Or, it diminishes us because we have not seen its intended purpose and accepted it. I hope that readers of this book will learn to laugh when suffering comes, knowing that suffering can be a gift from God.

James also calls us to living a servant life and demonstrates servanthood in his own life. He instructs us in the meaning of genuine faith and tells us that real faith results in ministry to the poor, disenfranchised, downtrodden and needy people around us. He tells us that a controlled life is possible for all who have a close relationship with God. It is in our relationship with God that our imaginations are captured. Captivation results in a changed inner being, which emanates into behavior that is real and not contaminated by human efforts. James helps his readers to understand the difference between real Christianity and plastic Christianity. He tells us that God has already placed qualities within us that need to be awakened. All who yearn for true greatness should benefit from the study of James.

God's Servant

Scripture reading: James 1:1. *This letter is from James, a servant of God and of the Lord Jesus Christ. It is written to Jewish Christians scattered among the nations. Greetings!*

James, Jesus' brother, was really God's servant. We need to honestly ask ourselves: Are we really God's servants? Or, do we just claim to be? Relentless self-honesty might reveal that this is just another false claim. However, it could be realistic, for enough of the deep within us can be captivated by the allure of God's character to assure that we will eventually be God's servants and we are already marked and destined for His service. We are seldom at our best and we often falter miserably, but God lovingly accepts us as we are. God loves us and permits incomplete followers of Jesus upon His team. This may make it difficult for us to evaluate our own authenticity, for we may see God's acceptance as affirmation that we are already mature Christians. Regardless, when we are captivated by something that will not let us go, God welcomes us into His family, knowing that when this captivation has produced its intended effect, like James, we will be servants of God and of the Lord Jesus Christ. Isn't it

1

amazing that God takes us as we are and begins to work toward our restoration and fulfillment?

My Prayer: Oh God, I am amazed that you do not seem to mind where I begin, for you specialize in my restoration. And when your captivation has produced its effect, like James, I will be a servant of God and of the Lord Jesus Christ. Father, your being has captured something deep within me, and it will not let me go. Thank you!

The Beauty of Servant Life

Scripture reading: James 1:1 (partial). *"...a servant of God..."*

Today, I reflect on servant life so that I may learn to appreciate its beauty. In humanity's quest for a quality life, the power and control kind of life appeals to most people; yet, it returns to us the least satisfaction. On the other hand, God saw that the servant life regenerates itself. This is why God made servanthood His choice for the essence of His being. And God was rewarded by the kind of life that is eternal by its nature. Do you see the reason why? The servant life lifts the served and the server. The power-control life diminishes both. God chose servant life and this distinguishes Him and validates Him as having the right to be God. It is our choice of servant life that inducts us into His Kingdom. How can we avoid the appeal of power and control, which appeals to most people? We will reject power and control when another kind of life captures our imaginations. And how does that captivation happen? It begins when we see the beauty in Jesus and invite Him to live in us. Eventually the beauty in Him will get hold of us like nothing else can. This is why Jesus is the Way.

My Prayer: Oh God, is it really more fulfilling to serve than to be served? Both must be exhilarating. Father, it is not easy to make servanthood my choice. Help me to see the beauty of your kind of life so that I may recognize its superiority and make it my choice.

Spontaneous Servanthood

Scripture reading: James 1:1 (partial). *"...James, a servant of God and of the Lord Jesus Christ..."*

I can try to mimic the servant life, but can I truly be a servant without Jesus' captivating influence upon me? Is it possible for us to become captivated by God's servant kind of life? Jesus walks with us so that we may experience the captivation that will transform our innermost beings into a nature that spontaneously embraces servanthood. I know that it's a lengthy walk and a slow process, but God doesn't give up. We can rejoice in our partial success and be happy to say with God's servant James, the Apostle, "I am a servant of God and of the Lord Jesus Christ." Are we being honest in wanting God to walk with us? Are we honestly willing to repent for walking alone for so long? Is there a relationship between honesty and servanthood? A still, small voice within whispers, "Yes, absolutely, for relentless self-honesty produces the repentance that will motivate us from within to spontaneously embrace servant life."

My Prayer: Father, forgive me for being such a slow learner, but I do see beauty in servanthood and I thank you for the lesson.

Many Changes

Scripture reading: James 1:1. *"From: James, a servant of God and of the Lord Jesus Christ. To: Jewish Christians scattered everywhere. Greetings!"*

Imagine having your brother proclaim Himself the Son of God. Then come to realize that He really is! Isn't it fascinating to think about the complete turnaround of James from the time just before Jesus' death when he didn't believe, (John 7:5), untill he wrote this practical book on Christian discipleship. In John 7:5 the scripture says, *"For even his brothers didn't believe him."* Can you and I experience changes in our understanding of and relationship with Jesus? Yes, James did and so may we! Is James' turnaround common to all who associate with Jesus? It absolutely is!

My Prayer: Lord, should I expect many changes in my life since I have invited you to live in and through me? I feel there is something about living intimately with you that brings the part of you already within me to the surface. For a time I thought it was not working, but ultimately I have come to believe that it really is. Thank you, dear God, that I am no longer the same, and my turnaround must be attributed to your presence in my life. Thank you, Lord Jesus, for invading my life and staying there even though I am a slow learner who mistreats you.

Unity and Community

Scripture reading: James 1:1 (partial). *"...To: Jewish Christians scattered everywhere. Greetings!"*

I am wondering, "When did James overcome his unbelief and become such a devoted follower of Jesus, his brother?" It must have happened during those years of persecution and hardship in Jerusalem. That persecution became a strong incentive toward unity and community. James was a leader and intimate member of the Jerusalem Christian fellowship. It is in the heat of hardship that *koinonia** emerges. This letter was written after the persecution of Christians in Jerusalem triggered the scattering of Christians who fled to avoid it. That fellowship experienced bonding that welded them into a community, which exploded in growth, and many strong Christians came from that greenhouse for spiritual growth and development. Would you like to be a participant in such fellowship? Our problem is: We want to have such unity without going through the stress that produces it. I doubt that such a pipe dream is possible. *Koinonia* (Christians bonded by kinship and fellowship into a family) has a price tag. In a prior experiment to achieve *koinonia*, I discovered that I, along with others, was not always capable of paying the price. However, our partial success has been a rewarding and stimulating venture into growth.

My Prayer: Father, there is so much healing that needs to occur within me. Will I ever experience unity and community like that experienced by James? My weakness prevents me from entering into close relationships and those relationships are essential to the healing of my weakness. I feel boxed in! Help me!! The reply that I hear is, "I am."

Koinonia is a transliteration of a Greek word for which we have no English equivalent. We do not have words to express this level of intimacy, so the only way to understand *koinonia* is to see it, then experience it. Even soldiers who train together and fight for their lives together are not bonded equivalent to this. This becomes not a closed society but an open society. Only those who hold on to their own barriers of separation will be excluded.

How may we achieve Christian *koinonia*? 1). You come to see its beauty and benefit. Then you want it. 2). You ask God for it. 3). You select a brother or sister (soul partners) and begin to lower any barriers separating you. 4). You spend time together (lots of time). 5). You learn how to love and be loved by another. Your reward is: You are there for each other when pain comes, and you will never again have to be or feel alone. The cost is: whatever happens to your soul partners affects you. Our selfish concern about our pain and discomfort prevents us from pursuing what James and early Christians had. But, avoiding *koinonia* also has its cost—it leaves us alone in a stressful world. Also we lose the spiritual growth and vitality that distinguished the early Christians.

Laugh at Trouble

Scripture reading: James 1:2 (partial). *"Dear brothers, is your life full of difficulties and temptations? Then be happy."*

Do you feel the warmth of James, this spiritual leader, flowing through the centuries to greet you? The stress that James went through during those early years of persecution and confusion contributed to his stature. We might feel that James is speaking to us and to all Christians who aspire to greatness. In verse 2, James says, *"Dear brothers, is your life full of difficulties and temptations? Then be happy."* I would resent those directions except I know that James has already been there. He has earned the right to prescribe for others by taking the medicine himself. As I review the difficulties of my past, I see little of the happiness that James prescribes because much of my energy is expended doing what James says that I should not do—trying to squirm out of my problems. Yet, now I see the fruit that those difficulties produced, and I am grateful for the challenges and the growth that came from them.

My Prayer: Father, may the spirit of your servant James flow down through the ages and rest upon me so that I, too, may laugh at trouble.

When Life Tumbles In

Scripture reading: James 1:2 & 3. *"Dear brothers, is your life full of difficulties and temptations? Then be happy, for when the way is rough, your patience has a chance to grow."*

James makes me uncomfortable, for I prefer comfort and ease before growth in godliness. I have to keep reminding myself that adversity can be a friend. This does not mean that I am to court disaster. However, when life tumbles in, I am to view this as another opportunity to have the God that is already within me stirred, brought to the surface, and become a fixed feature of my character. We need enough trials to make us strong, enough sorrow to keep us human, and enough hope to make us thirsty for God's kind of life. I saw this demonstrated by my mentor, Nat Tracy. When he and his wife were told that his liver cancer was not treatable, they went home and prayed that they might take this and make something beautiful from it. What I saw in both of them was beautiful!

My Prayer: Father, I ask that I may learn to take the adversities that befall me and make something beautiful from them.

Patience

Scripture reading: James 1:3. *"...For when the way is rough, your patience has a chance to grow."*

When I think of patience, I think of someone who can afford to wait. Apparently, James considered this virtue to be of huge importance in a spiritual journey. I wonder, why? It could be that the magnitude of what God is doing in us requires patience. Such an enterprise cannot be accomplished quickly. If we allow impatience to dominate us, we will short circuit the process—setting back the whole enterprise. Patience is an expression of our faith in God who has promised to infuse new life into us. Our impatience is a signal that we do not yet fully trust God—our patience enables God to take us and mold us into the creatures He wants us to become. Yet, we live in a world that is saturated with impatience—instant gratification, fast foods, and a work environment that often demands instant response from us. Somewhere we need to learn the discipline of patience. Could James be right? Could we learn patience when the way is rough?

My Prayer: Father, I am not asking for adversity, but help me to take those adversities that befall me as an opportunity to have patience instilled within me, which will be the beginning of growth in godliness.

Problems–A Threat or a Gift?

Scripture reading: James 1:3&4 (partial). *"...For when the way is rough, your patience has a chance to grow. So let it grow, and don't try to squirm out of your problems..."*

Why is it difficult to accept adversity as an opportunity to experience growth? We should know by now that it is a key to our growth. The way we deal with adversity determines the way that adversity will deal with us. Adversity can make us, or it can break us. Our attitude toward it is the pivotal point. When we view problems not as a threat, but as a gift, we will have boldness to take risks and live on an edge. Such a position will bring adventure, excitement, and growth into our lives. Yet, even when we intellectually know this, we continue to try to squirm out of our problems without being grateful for the opportunity to be expanded. Why? Could it be that smooth sailing is of more value to us than growth in godliness?

My Prayer: Oh God, when will the beauty of your kind of life appeal to me more than a safe harbor? Could it be that I have yet to see the beauty in you and love it enough to pay any price in order to have it? Father, I do not want to be a wimp! I do not want to live life with nothing but safety in view! I want to really live! The reply that I hear is, **"Then stop trying to squirm out of your problems and accept them as an opportunity for expansion."**

Ready for Anything

Scripture reading: James 1:4 (partial). *"...For when your patience is finally in full bloom, then you will be ready for anything, strong in character, full and complete."*

In the beginning of my spiritual pilgrimage, I aspired to become a mature Christian, but now I aspire to become a maturing Christian. However, there is a sense in which we can be where we should be at the moment. We may still long for the promise of strong character and a full and complete being, but if we cannot totally achieve such being at this moment, we can at least be on the way toward it. Yet, I moan when it becomes apparent to me that I grieve God by remaining less than I am and could be.

My Prayer: Father, will I ever be all that I can be? The answer that I hear is, **"No, for your being is infinitum."**

Recognizing God's Voice

Scripture reading: James 1:5 (partial). *"If you want to know what God wants you to do, ask him..."*

I do, but other voices disguise themselves as God's voice, and I find it hard to discern between them. Is it ever going to become easier for me to recognize God's voice? I am sorry that I do not always get it right. There is a little dog named Patches that belongs to one of the patients at the nursing home where my wife's father resides. Pat, my wife, has always loved dogs, and they always love her. Whenever Patches hears Pat's voice, she recognizes it and comes running to Pat. I wish that I had Patches' gift for recognizing meaningful voices. Perhaps herein lies the key: The more meaningful someone becomes to us, the better tuned we become to the sound of his or her voice.

My Prayer: Father, would you help me to draw near to you so that you become dear to me and I can then recognize your voice? (This is an, "Ah-ha", in my life!) Father, is it in loving you that your voice will become recognizable? If this is so, I ask that you give to me a revelation of yourself that will capture the deep within me and enlist love that I cannot conjure up alone. The reply that I hear is, **"Do you understand what you are asking?"** *And I reply, "I think I do." And God responds,* **"OK!"**

Am I A Misfit?

Scripture reading: James 1:8 (partial). *"...If you don't ask with faith, don't expect the Lord to give you any solid answer."*

I feel somewhat jerked about by James. First of all, James tells me, *"If you want to know what God wants you to do, ask him, and he will gladly tell you",* then he states, *"...If you don't ask with faith, don't expect the Lord to give you any solid answer."* What should I do when my hearing is faulty and my faith is weak? Shall I ask anyway and hope to blunder through to an answer? The reply that I hear is, *"Yes."*

My Prayer: Father, learning to walk in step with your spirit has not been an easy lesson for me. Am I a misfit? Do any of your other children have difficulties like this? The reply, *"Do they ever! Many are not as honest as you and will not acknowledge, even to themselves, that they are struggling. I am pleased that you seek my will even without faith. And don't worry about your struggle, I have taken a special interest in your development, and I'll get you where you need to be."*

Core Values

Scripture reading: James 1:7. *"For let not that man think that he shall receive any thing of the Lord."*(KJV)

James is referring to the person who cannot ask in faith. He continues to say in James 1:8, (KJV): *"A double minded man is unstable in all his ways."* Is our faith in proportion to the level of our understanding of God and appreciation for Him? "Yes!" We are value-animated beings and we do not always have our values in their proper order. This fractures us and makes us unstable. The penalty for our failure to recognize God's beauty is an unsettled core that will sabotage the desires of our hearts, (core values). Will this cause us to ask for and pray for things that are not in our best interest? "Yes!" God is not under obligation to provide us with those things that we ask for under such conditions. In effect, it is not God denying what we ask for—we deny them to ourselves by asking amiss. The key here is to have the desires of our hearts rearranged, then our prayers will be only for that which is best for us.

My Prayer: God, can I depend upon you to always give what I ask for under such correct conditions? A voice within responds, **"You can depend upon it!!"** *Father, am I seeing this right? Does my inability to* *see you clearly prevent me from loving you? Does my failure to love you stem the faith that I should have, but do not have? Does my unstable core deny me the blessings that I desire? If the answers to these questions are;" yes", then it becomes important to have my core values in their proper order, isn't it? Father, I cannot reach deep inside me to flip the switch that will change the core values that are within me. I must have help and you are the only adequate source for such help. Reach inside me and reorder my values. The reply: "James, you are a complicated being. I am getting you there just as fast as I can".*

Material Values

Scripture reading: James 1:9-10. *"Let the brother of low degree rejoice in that he is exalted: But the rich, in that he is made low: because as the flower of the grass he shall pass away." (KJV).*

Affluence may be desired, but it should not be the ruling passion of our core values. Valuing matter is not detrimental, but making the material our primary value is. We cannot change our values. We do not rule them; they rule us. When the God-kind of life came into the world in the man Jesus, the world was shaken. Are we trapped without hope? "No," when that same kind of life enters our lives, we will also be shaken. Jesus takes us as His assignment. The task of reordering our values is His work, not ours. It is not an easy task. But, His abiding love eventually stirs the core of our beings and brings change there that we could never accomplish without Him. Remember, God does this for us even though we have caused Him great sorrow and pain.

My Prayer: Father, I am impatient for captivation that will cause all the values within me to fall into their proper order. Is Jesus going to get this done?

The answer, "He will get it done! But so large a task must be taken over a long period of time for it to be permanent and real. We are going to do this right or not at all. And when we are finished, Lucifer will no longer be able to sway you." I breathe deeply and sigh, "Thank you."

Love The Right Self

Scripture reading: James 1:11 (partial). *"...They will soon die and leave behind all their busy activities."*

This is a continuation of James' warning to those who allow the material to become their primary value. James warns us that, in such a scenario, death will separate us from that which we treasure most. What can we value that will not be left behind? It is that which we can still have beyond death—it is ourselves. The person that we become is all that we will take with us when we depart this life. Does this mean that we are to value ourselves? That is correct. But, is this not self-love? Yes, it is, but self-love is acceptable as long as we love the right self. We were made in the image of God—His imprint is stamped within us. When we come to love God's kind of life, those imprints spring to life and become the foundation for our character. Our character, (spirit) is all that we will carry with us when we depart this life.

My Prayer: Father, it is important for me to love you and the imprint of your image within me, isn't it? The reply that I hear is, **"Absolutely!"**

Temptation

Scripture reading: James 1:12 (partial). *"Happy is the man who doesn't give in and do wrong when he is tempted..."*

The Lord's Prayer ends with a request, *"And don't let us yield to temptation,"* (Luke 11:4, NLT). Sometimes, I don't give in to temptation, and sometimes I do. When I don't do so, I am rewarded with feelings of accomplishment and self-worth, which reinforce my character. When I do give in to temptation, I have feelings of failure and self-hate, which are very self-destructive. This reward-punishment response can be beneficial to my progress. However, it is not just our behavior that God is targeting. He is targeting our very being, out of which our behavior flows. It would be a mistake to rearrange our behavior and leave the innermost being untouched. You and I cannot live rightly on our own. Our own strength is not sufficient to deal with temptation. We need God, and He is readily available to all who call upon Him.

My Prayer: Father, I am too complicated a being to ever extract myself from the mess that I am. I place myself in your trust and wait for the redemption that you have promised. The response that I hear is, **"You have made a wise choice."**

The Evil Within

Scripture reading: James 1:14. *"Temptation is the pull of man's own evil thoughts and wishes."*

When an evil thought comes to my mind, I honestly ask, "Where did that come from?" It did not fall from the sky, and some demonic agent did not put it there. It came from within me. It is hard to admit that such a distasteful inner being resides in me. Whenever I hear stories of inhumanities perpetrated upon people, I feel for both the victimized person and the perpetrator; for I know that, without God's intervention, it could have been I who victimizes others. And I know that factors other than strength of character keep the beast at bay within others and me. For instance: fear of exposure or punishment, cultural practices, guilt from past forays, fear of retaliation, desire for approval, and cowardice, to name a few. This means that I have a kinship to every human being; the same distasteful life that resides in them resides in me. But never let me forget that the imprint of God's hand resides in each of us too. We are brothers.

My Prayer: Father, will the evil that resides within me ever be put away? The answer, **"It most certainly will! And steps have already been taken to guarantee it."**

God Chose Me!

Scripture reading: James 1:18. *"And it was a happy day for him when he gave us our new lives, through the truth of his Word, and we became, as it were, the first children in his new family."*

It stretches my mind to fathom the enterprise that God has undertaken. He is going to demonstrate the superiority of His love-servant kind of life by inducting wayward people like us into his family. This demonstration will convince even the rebelling angels that the love-servant life deserves to be supreme. And then, the rift that occurred among these beings, before the foundation of the world was laid, will be healed. I need the freedom to honestly evaluate myself. I need to see and recognize what an illegitimate and wayward being I really am. Without such recognition I will have difficulty appreciating the grace of God. Whenever I honestly contemplate just how crippled we are, I am compelled to appreciate the character of God. For His vocation is taking cripples such as us and fashioning new beings that are capable of governing the cosmos with Him.

My Prayer: Father, it is a good plan, but I can hardly believe that you would choose me to be a member of your family. The answer that I hear is, **"Believe it!"**

The Word of God

Scripture reading: James 1:18 (partial). *"...Through the truth of his Word."*

God's love-servant life is an expression of who God is and what He is like. When we see and hear that expression, it should capture the deep within us. Some translations capitalize 'Word', for it is understood to be a synonym for the person, Jesus, who fleshed God's character for us. When I heard with some understanding that God was demonstrating the superiority of His kind of life by offering that same kind of life to wayward persons like myself, something leaped inside of me to respond to that offer. James 1:18 now has meaning for me, *"Of his own will begat he us with the word of truth, that we should be a kind of first fruits of his creatures."* (KJV). If the offer that the Godhead has made (to infuse their kind of life into us) does not capture our imaginations and draw us into a pilgrimage, there is nothing better that God has to offer that will appeal to us.

My Prayer: Father, if such an act does not get hold of me, nothing else will! Don't allow this offer to escape me! The answer that I hear is, **"don't you allow this** *offer to escape you!"* I respond, *"But left with my own resources to do this perfectly, I will mess up!"* The reply, *"All you need to do is to become excited about becoming a person like me, then I will see to it that you do not mess up!"* *I wipe the sweat from my brow and sigh, "Thank you!"*

Anger

Scripture reading: James 1:19 (KJV). *"Wherefore, my beloved brethren, let every man be swift to hear, slow to speak, slow to wrath:"*

I did not realize how much influence James had upon my life until I carefully read this verse again. I must acknowledge that only two-thirds of these admonitions have been easy for me. I listen well and I am very careful about what I say, but anger rages within me. The anger that I suppressed during my childhood has found fertile soil in which to grow. And it has grown! The discovery of God's forgiveness, being forgiven, and learning to forgive others and myself are the antidotes for this dilemma. God's forgiveness inspires me to forgive those who have harmed me. The most difficult accomplishment is coming to forgive myself for the hostility that I harbored toward those who bruised me.

My Prayer: Father, without your help, my anger would have expanded until there was an explosion. Thank you for helping me. The reply that I hear is, **"It was my pleasure!"**

Healing of The Inner Life

Scripture reading: James 1:21. *"So get rid of all that is wrong in your life, both inside and outside, and humbly be glad for the wonderful message we have received, for it is able to save our souls as it takes hold of our hearts."*

There is a difference between hearing a message and getting a message. There is an, "Ah-ha!" that goes along with getting a message. Healing of my inner life is not a self-effort accomplishment. It is something that flows from the, "Ah-has!" along the way.

My Prayer: Father, am I getting a message that will take hold of my heart and heal me from within? The answer, **"James, at one time you did not have the foggiest idea of what the Good News is all about. Now, you have an inkling of understanding. But, the whole picture still awaits you. If you keep hanging around, you are going to be caught by something that will not let you go."** *I respond, "I hope so."*

Looking Good Versus Being Good

Scripture reading: James 1:21 (partial). *"...both inside and outside..."*.

There is a strong temptation to resist changes in our inner lives. Subsequently, we major only upon external re-arrangement of our lives. For every external flaw in my life there is an internal cause. Spiritual healing within will naturally flow into my external life. I saw this reality demonstrated while serving for five years as chaplain for the Texas Youth Council's statewide juvenile reception and assessment center. These juveniles were acting out the inner mess that they and others had made. Rehabilitation programs major primarily upon behavior modification. These programs encourage external re-arrangement of one's life. In many of our churches, we do the same. I think that it is time that we followed Jesus' admonition to the Pharisees, to clean the inside of the cup (Matt.23: 25-26). If we will not do this, then, like the Pharisees, we will become whitewashed tombs.

My Prayer: Father, save me from the temptation to look good! And bring me to the position of being good!

It Automatically Happens

Scripture reading: James 1:22 (partial). *"And remember, it is a message to obey, not just to listen to."*

James is referring back to verse 21 where He talks about the message that takes hold of our hearts. When we get the message, we can trust the deep within us to respond. We have been made so that this automatically happens. We do not have to rev up our RPMs to assure a response. We should not worry about the response; it will take care of itself. Our concern should be about getting the message. When we discover the magnitude of what God has done, this act of God will reveal a being of compelling beauty. Getting the message captivates our innermost being and draws us into a spiritual journey. Believe it! My head and my heart began to listen when I was 8 years old (I am now 76 years old) has this message taken root within my heart? Yes, it has! The heart response does not take long: it is the spiritual journey that goes on forever!

My Prayer: Father, I praise you for choosing the kind of life that compels my heart to take notice!

Honesty With Myself

Scripture reading: James 1:22 (partial). *"...So don't fool your-selves."*

The separation of our head from our heart has made it possible for us to be something entirely different from the way that we see ourselves. Such disunity hides the dark side of our inner life and discourages the remorse and sense of urgency necessary to promote our spiritual pilgrimage. James describes such a person as, *"...as soon as he walks away, he can't see himself anymore or remember what he looks like."* (James 1:23 & 24 (partial).

My Prayer: Father, will your compelling beauty reveal your love and forgiveness, which enables me to be honest in my self-evaluation? When I am equipped with the assurance of your forgiveness, may I then enter into the deepest recesses of my heart and see and admit to myself the kind of person that I really am? And when I am free to do this, will I experience a uniting of my head with my heart so that unity and wholeness are returned to me? And will the wholeness that results from this make even the sky not to be a limit to the person I may then become? Father, the burden is not just upon me, is it? It is upon the beauty of your being and my ability

*to see it. Open the eyes of my heart to see who you are!
Father God replies,* "I am infinitely more, but you can be sure that Jesus is like me. I have done my best by sending my Son for you to examine. Seek Him, know Him, and you will be seeing the beauty of my character that has the ability to capture your heart and carry you where you alone are not able to go."

Free to Look Inside

Scripture reading: James 1:25. *"But if anyone keeps looking steadily into God's law for free men, he will not only remember* **it**, *but he will do what* **it** *says, and God will greatly bless him in everything he does."*

What is the **'it'**? **'It'** is a reference to God's law for free men. But what is that? In verse 21, James talks about a wonderful message that we have received that can take hold of our hearts. James does not connect the dots well here, but it appears that God's law for free men and this wonderful message are the same. James assumes that all readers will know what he is talking about, but that is not always the case. James' silence places upon us the responsibility of determining the content of God's law for free men and the wonderful message that we have received. I interpret this wonderful message as: God demonstrating the superiority of His life by sharing His kind of life with all those who respond to it. Our Sin is not an obstacle between God and us. His forgiveness takes care of our Sin. Armed with the forgiveness of God, we are free to look into the recesses of our beings where we will find the kind of life that is advocated by God's adversary. And we discover that God's loving kind of life is our only hope for escaping this life of death, for it will be the beauty of God's being that lures us into His kind of life and frees us. Also, the journey inward will reveal the imprint of God's hand within us, and the beauty that is potentially ours when we are free.

My Prayer: Father, am I really free to look inside and see who I actually am? Must I fear what I will find? The reply I hear is, **"You are free! And you do not have to be afraid!"**

Personality Murder

Scripture reading: James 1:26 (partial). *"Anyone who says he is a Christian but doesn't control his sharp tongue is just fooling himself..."*

Our tongues can be a weapon we use in the slaughter of persons. Personality murder is the most prevalent form of murder. We perform these murders with words and attitudes. We should recognize that persons in our circle of acquaintances sense our assessment of them, and they are made more alive by our attitudes toward them or they are made less alive. Words can be the stabbing darts that we throw to bring harm upon other persons. Our selection of God's kind of life and invitation to Jesus to enter our lives to help us should stem the flow of negative attitudes and stinging words flowing out of us. It is not possible for us to reach deep into our innermost beings and change attitudes, but we can place ourselves in a position for God to change them for us. That position may be described as putting ourselves into God's hands. If personality murder does not cease, then we are fooling ourselves about the sincerity of our choice of God's kind of life.

My Prayer: Father, I do not want to be self-deceived. Help me to find the freedom that will allow me to see what is in my own heart! Give me honest brothers and sisters who will lovingly help me to see myself honestly.

Authentic Christianity

Scripture reading: James 1:27 (partial). *"The Christian who is pure and without fault, from God the Father's point of view, is the one who takes care of orphans and widows..."*

Authentic Christians are always evidenced by service to the disenfranchised, downtrodden, poor and needy people around them*. Even then, we are capable of doing those services for the sake of appearances, without genuine concern for these people. Only God can deliver us from the dark side that resides within us and transform us into authentic Christians. How much service do I render to the disenfranchised, downtrodden, poor and needy? I should hang my head in shame. I am the loser. Nothing lifts my spirit and opens my eyes as much as service to the needy. My own cleansing is accomplished in the midst of service. Serving others is the path, if I want to be pure and without fault.

My Prayer: Lord Jesus, come quickly and deliver me!

*A modern interpretation by Aristides describing Christians to the Emperor Hadrian in about 125 A.D.

"They love one another. They never fail to help widows; they save orphans from those who would hurt them. If they have something, they give freely to the man who has nothing; if they see a stranger, they take him home, and are happy, as though he were a real brother. They don't consider themselves brothers in the usual sense, but brothers instead through the Spirit, in God."

Anemic Churches

Scripture reading: James 1:27 (partial). *"...not soiled and dirtied by his contacts with the world."*

James is talking about the Christian who is pure. In our time, anemic Christianity has become so prevalent that it is accepted as the norm. In our Western culture, with Plato's image of man, we tend to see man as a trichotomy of body, mind and spirit and not as a unity of body, mind and spirit. This allows us to attempt to give our souls to God for His safekeeping while trying to hold on to the remainder of ourselves for ourselves. It is like trying to give someone an egg by giving him or her just the shell, leaving the remaining egg white and egg yoke to fall apart. This adds to the disunity that already exists within us. It encourages the division between our head and our heart. If authentic Christianity is to appear in our culture, there must arise a potent, dynamic movement that only God can accomplish. Our renewal efforts are destined to fail. In the 1960's a counter-revolution sprang up to counter the cultural revolution of that era. This counter-revolution took shape as a spiritual renewal movement. I was part of this counter-revolution and quite certain that within two or three years I would inspire vibrant churches across our land. I did not, for I was too much a product of the anemic church that had formed me, and the task was much too difficult for human efforts alone.

My Prayer: Father, I ask that you will do something special in me and the church that will break the stranglehold of spiritual anemia.

Leaking Values

Scripture reading: James 2:1. *"Dear brothers, how can you claim that you belong to the Lord Jesus Christ, the Lord of glory, if you show favoritism to rich people and look down on poor people?"*

James poses a good question. Our values are leaked in unsuspecting ways. Our choice of friends and associates will reveal what values reside in us. Yet, neither are we to show favoritism to the poor and look down on rich people. If we are to be authentic Christians, then we should hold all persons, rich or poor, in high esteem. It was this quality about Jesus that endeared Him to both the rich and the poor. We will be broader persons if we have associates in all situations of life, for every person holds qualities that could be infused into us and enrich us.

My Prayer: Father, teach me to hold all persons in high esteem and enrich my life by those qualities in everyone, so that my own being will be expanded.

Wrong Again

Scripture reading: James 2:4. *"Judging a man by his wealth shows that you are guided by wrong motives."*

While I was a college student, I tutored the son of a rich family. I saw faults and weaknesses in this family that made loving and appreciating them difficult for me. Consequently, I had a tendency to despise the rich. I got it wrong again! While serving on a mission in Africa, I was viewed by the Nationals as a rich person. I was concerned that they might view me as I viewed this rich family.

My Prayer: Father, help me to see persons and not wealth or poverty.

Blessed Are The Poor

Scripture reading: James 2:5 (partial). *"Listen to me, dear brothers: God has chosen poor people to be rich in faith..."*

Does God favor poor people? No, there is something about poverty that draws poor people near to God. Physical helplessness may call our attention to our spiritual helplessness and prompt us to seek God. Affluence may draw us into affordable pursuits that draw us away from God. It appears that the rich may have spiritual struggles that the poor do not have. If this is true, then those of less affluence should be thankful. At the same time, the affluent who successfully find closeness to God should be respected.

My Prayer: Father, teach me to respect and value person who are spiritually mature, with or without affluence.

Living in Another Domain

Scripture reading: James 2:5 (partial). *"...The Kingdom of Heaven is theirs, for that is the gift God has promised to all those who love him."*

A kingdom is a domain where a set of laws and principles rule and obtain, and keeping those laws and principles rewards us with valuable returns. God already lives by these laws and principles, and He experiences the kind of life that is delightful and productive. We may live by them too. But the rebellious kind of life that already resides within us will not allow us to do that until we come to love God sufficiently to spontaneously and willingly submit to those laws and principles. So, God presents Himself to us in a form that we can love. God's kind of life comes to us as a baby born in a barn. He grew into a man that we can see, understand and love. When we love Jesus, we love God, and as our reward we are drawn and privileged to live in a domain of laws and principles that only the spiritually elite may live by.

My Prayer: Father, Thank You! I could never have made this transition without such simple help! Thank You! Thank You! Thank You!

Made for The God Kind of Life

Scripture reading: James 2:8. *"Yes indeed, it is good when you truly obey our Lord's command, you must love and help your neighbors just as much as you love and take care of yourself."*

I cannot honestly claim to be such a person, yet I see and proclaim its value, but accomplishing it escapes me. The life of God's adversary has taken root deeply within me and refuses to easily die. I was not made to live the adversary's way. I was made for the God kind of life. Yet, I appear to be stuck with a kind of life that displeases me and leaves me without rewards. Why?

My Prayer: Father, why am I stuck with a kind of life that is distasteful to me? The answer, **"Because I want you to be sure that you will never want to go back to such impoverished living! So I am going to let you rub your nose in the kind of life that displeases you until you become so disgusted that you would never go back to such life for all eternity. "**

God Loves the Guilty

Scripture reading: James 2:10. *"And the person who keeps every law of God, but makes one little slip, is just as guilty as the person who has broken every law there is."*

Must we never break any of God's laws? I hope that this is not the case! If it is, we are all goners! This passage is not about our final destiny, but about our guilt. Are we guilty of breaking some of God's laws? Absolutely!! Are we guilty for the slightest slip? Yes, just as guilty as those who trample God's laws underfoot. It is we who make guilt or innocence an issue in our final destiny, and our final destiny is not even the focus here. The focus is on who we are and who we are becoming.

Clint Eastwood has this line in the motion picture, *Unforgiven*; "We all deserve to be shot." God seems to have an affinity for the guilty. Therefore, we are prime candidates for response to and relationship with God. And it is that combination of a response and a relationship with God that will determine our ultimate destiny, not our guilt or innocence!

My Prayer: Father, I want to switch my focus from; where I will be to who I am becoming. Could I have some help here? The reply I hear is, **"Yes!"**

47

Behavior Matters

Scripture reading: James 2:12 (partial). *"...So watch what you do and what you think."*

In the previous meditation, it could have been interpreted that our behavior (guilt or innocence) does not matter. It does matter. Our behavior is the mirror reflecting who we are. And the world has already been constituted as a place where we will receive similar treatment for that which we give.

God's love for the guilty may be seen in the principle of the innocent suffering for the sins of the guilty. It was God's love for the guilty that prompted Him to create a world in which innocents suffer because of others' guilt. It is God's hope that this added pain would prompt the guilty to change. The suffering of innocents for the sins of the guilty becomes an added incentive to be careful about what we do and think. If we were creating the world, we probably would not create it where innocents must suffer for the sins of the guilty, but we are not God and we do not love the guilty as He loves them.

My Prayer: Father, I do not want to receive in proportion to what I give. However, since the world is programmed to respond that way, help me to be careful about what I give. And never let me forget that when I sin, others suffer because of my sin.

Pseudo Christianity

Scripture reading: James 2:14. *"Dear brothers, what's the use of saying that you have faith and are Christians if you aren't proving it by helping others? Will that kind of faith save anyone?"*

Good question! We should always be clear in our presentation of the doctrine of salvation by grace through faith. Authentic faith is always accompanied by a change in behavior. The Western culture's immersion in Plato's image of man as a trichotomy instead of a unity allows people to think they can give their souls to God for safekeeping while holding on to the remainder of their selves. This coupled with the concept that any kind of faith is saving faith has produced a community of pseudo Christians masquerading as authentic Christians. But they may not be! We should feel sorry for such self-deceived persons who will be surprised in a final judgment.

My Prayer: Father, awaken all contemporary churchmen and me to a frightening reality: Many who wear the brand of Christianity are not genuine, and are at risk.

Useless Faith

Scripture reading: James 2:17 (partial). *"...Faith that doesn't show itself by good works is no faith at all–it is dead and useless."*

Again, "authentic faith" is always accompanied by a change in behavior. This needs to be affirmed over and over. We who operate under cheap grace and pseudo faith need to have our conscience awakened. It was Dietrich Bonhoffer who startled my conscience when he claimed that the proclamation of cheap grace was the reason that German Christians could sit comfortably in their pews while Hitler murdered six million Jews and countless other disenfranchised German citizens. Bonhoffer's faith was not dead or useless. He could have safely stayed in the U.S. but returned to Germany to continue his opposition to Hitler's régime. Consequently, Bonhoffer was arrested and put in prison. He was executed when Hitler made a late war and last minute decision to retaliate against all his enemies.

My Prayer: Father, when the disciples asked Jesus, "Am I the one who will betray you?" He could have replied, "You all will!" Faith to really believe does not come to me easily. Is my weak faith a betrayal of Jesus? The reply that I hear is, "Yes, it is!"

Authentic Faith

Scripture reading: James 2:20 (partial). *"Fool! When will you ever learn that "believing" is useless without doing what God wants you to?"*

Has James made his point? Are we ready for James to move forward to something else? Why does James' persistence upon making this point irritate us? It could be because hearing that authentic faith always results in a change of behavior is threatening to us.

My Prayer: Father, faith is your gift to all those who are drawn near enough to Jesus to see His character and recognize its beauty and superiority. It is not enough for me to just intellectually know this. I must be drawn to Jesus for authentic faith to spring to life within me. So, draw me to Him who is the author and finisher of my faith. The reply that I hear is, "I am."

Friends With God

Scripture reading: James 2:23 (partial). *"...Abraham trusted God, and the Lord declared him good in God's sight, and he was even called, 'the friend of God'."*

The unconditional forgiveness and acceptance of God permit us to draw near to Him. When we do so, we discover His marvelous being—His character. Or, is it the other way around? When we discover who God really is, we draw near to Him? It probably is the latter. Regardless, this discovery engenders our relationship and God becomes our friend. James' point is, "It becomes easier to do what God desires for us when we are friends."

My Prayer: Father, I want to become your friend. The reply that I hear is, **"That would please me a lot."**

New Vision

Scripture reading: James 2:26. *"Just as the body is dead when there is no spirit in it, so faith is dead if it is not the kind that results in good deeds."*

What is the kind of faith that does not result in good deeds? Apparently, it must be some kind of faith that does not result in a change of behavior. James does not mince words; he calls this "dead faith". I call it "pseudo faith". God's adversary is very clever, and he wants to maintain power and control over us. So the adversary's kind of life comes to reside in us. When we succumbed to this Sin (not just sins), it prompted us to substitute pseudo faith in the place of authentic faith. To do this, we separated our head from our heart, which allowed us to contentedly continue in such a divided state without even knowing what we were doing. If we are to be saved from such madness, we must have megatons of help here. And we have it! Our invitation to Jesus to reside within us, coupled with the awakened desire to live His kind of life, will ultimately heal our disunity. Then our head and heart will become united. When they are, it will be like another set of eyes being handed to us. This has been called, "seeing the light". This new vision of God and ourselves will combine to solidify a genuine faith within us, one very similar to

Abraham's obedience. This brings to us the wholeness that will allow us to function, as we were intended to function. It can happen! It is happening! This is what being saved is all about!

My Prayer: Father, thank you for saving me, (present tense).

Confrontation

Scripture reading: James 3:1 (partial). *"Dear brothers, don't be too eager to tell others their faults..."*

Good idea! Correcting others for their faults could, and often does, have repercussions. The only time that it seems to rectify rather than degrade is when there already exists a close relationship of accountability to one another. Even that can be jeopardized at times. Correcting the faults of others can be focusing away from our own. Jesus talked about trying to remove specks from the eyes of others when a fence post is sticking out of our own. Such does not set well with others. However, there are times when love dictates that we call our brothers', or sister's attention to an inconsistency. Even then, it must be done delicately and with finesse, and it is useless without genuine love.

My Prayer: Father, teach me to be silent when silence is best and confronting when that is best. Confrontation is the most difficult for me.

Consequences for Our Mistakes

Scripture reading: James 3:2 (partial). *"...for we all make many mistakes (sins)[1]; and when we teachers of religion, who should know better, do wrong, our punishment will be greater than it would be for others."*

Must we wait until we are perfect before confronting others over some concern we have about them? If that is the case, we will never be able to confront anyone. Our imperfection should not excuse us from being accountable for the growth and maturity of others. However, we are apt to allow our own lack of maturity to stand in the way. Moreover, what about the added punishment of which James speaks? Our image of God should not be that of a policeman who follows us around to strike us down for some wrong. Yet, there is a price to pay for our mistakes (sins); one that has already been programmed into the scope of the principles that govern our world. God is responsible for our punishment only in that He set in place those governing principles with consequences. We do not break these principles: we break ourselves by smashing into them. As a religious leader, my careless handling of those principles adds another

---

[1] Author's and Editor's interpretation

consequence, the consequence of taking lightly a leadership position.

My Prayer: Father, if I do not get everything right, will you love me anyway? The reply, "I will love you anyway, but that will not waive the consequences."

Life Taker or Life Giver?

Scripture reading: James 3:5 (partial). *"So also the tongue is a small thing, but what enormous damage it can do..."*

Our words are the vehicle that we use to transport ideas from our minds to the minds of others. Those ideas can be life giving or they can be life taking. If we are insecure, we may attempt to bring others down to soothe our own dissatisfaction with ourselves. Unless we are careful with our words, we may slaughter innocents for the sake of our own comfort, self-esteem, and aggrandizement. We need to take a close look at the scenario above: Hyper criticism is the work of an insecure person willing to commit personality murder of innocents for the sake of his or her need to feel better about him self or her self. Do we want to be such persons? Of course not! How may we avoid it? By exercising our will power to control our tongues? No! We avoid it by discovering the source of real security, which relieves us of the need to slaughter others in an attempt to sooth our feelings about ourselves.

Our tongues can also elevate others. Our words may not always be spoken, for we also telecommunicate with others by our attitudes. Sensing how we feel about them can elevate or diminish others. Therefore, we can become life takers or life givers.

I experienced this on a retreat at Kaleo Lodge in East Texas. These retreats usually begin on Friday night and close Sunday after lunch. During the login time, participants tell who they are, why they came, and what they hope to accomplish upon this retreat. A lady participant logged in saying; "I got to meet James Gibson this afternoon." My wife who was sitting beside me quietly moaned. This lady continued; "Now I know what God looks like." My wife burst out; "Oh no! Now I am going to have to live with him." This affirmation gave me courage, confidence, and a feeling of well-being. Sylvia Saunders affirmed me, and I became more alive.

My Prayer: Father, insecurity not only kills me, but also it prompts me to kill others. Help me to find the source of real security, and from that foundation my words will give life instead of taking it.

Control of Our Lives

Scripture reading: James 3:4. *"And a tiny rudder makes a huge ship turn wherever the pilot wants it to go, even though the winds are strong."*

Do we want to be in control of our lives and actions? Then, there must be something deep under girding us. The rudder of our lives is the being that resides deep within us. How may we get at something so deep and hidden? We cannot do this alone, but God can and wants to do this with us. Our sole contribution is to want to become such a person—a person who wants those qualities that God has already placed potentially within them to be awakened. But, what if we are so dead that we do not even want this? There is still hope. God hangs around and tantalizes the desires within us. He is like the salt that makes an unwilling horse want to go to water and drink.

My Prayer: Father, thank you for hanging around until I saw qualities in you that made me want to be like you. Would you awaken those passions within me that will animate me toward strength of being? The reply that I hear is, "I am already doing this and I will continue until the job is done."

Tame Me

Scripture reading: James 3:8 (partial) and 3:12 (partial). *"But no human being can tame the tongue...and you can't draw fresh water from a salty pool."*

Isn't it amazing that New Testament Christians were having trouble controlling their tongues? And isn't it amazing that after two thousand years we are still having this same problem? James was reminding them that inner strength of character is impossible to summon without help. However, a voice within keeps whispering, "You can do it yourself!" An adage that keeps popping up in email correspondence says, "Let go and let God." That's the position that will produce strength of character within us.

My Prayer: Father, tame me and freshen me as only you can!

Untangle Me

Scripture reading: James 3:16. *"For wherever there is jealousy or selfish ambition, there will be disorder and every other kind of evil."*

There is a price that we pay for refusing to allow God to tame and freshen our inner lives. That price is a disorderly life accented by evil, jealousy, and selfish ambitions. In the creation of an arena to test qualities of life, God set penalties to penalize those making wrong choices. Satan may have thought that this would be a good plan, for at that time I feel sure that he was absolutely certain that his preferred kind of life was supreme. So it may have been mutually acceptable to penalize anyone who persisted in any kind of life that is not supreme. If this scenario is valid, I wonder how many times Satan has wished that he had objected to those penalties. Those penalties are still in force, and they are not altogether bad for us. When we are in the penalty box, we have opportunity to examine the character choices that we are making and reconsider.

My Prayer: Father, if my life is to be untangled, I must have your help in taming and freshening my innermost being. The reply, "James, that is the way the world is pre-made and set: The prerequisite for an untangled life is an untangled inner being. Abide by my principles or pay the consequences."

The God-Kind of Life

Scripture reading: James 3:17 &18 (partial) *"...pure and full of quiet gentleness... peace loving and courteous... willing to yield to others...full of mercy and good deeds... wholehearted and straightforward and sincere...those who are peacemakers and will plant seeds of peace and reap a harvest of goodness."*

What is this innermost being that we have been referring to? When our innermost being is pure, it is defined as the God-kind of life, which is difficult to describe. We define the God-kind of life much like we define electricity. It is difficult to describe electricity, but it is easier to describe what it does. We may describe the God-kind of life in that same way—James describes it in terms of how it behaves and not in terms of what it is. We selfishly want the benefit of those qualities without the being that prompts them to flow from us. The problem is: We cannot have those benefits without the character that produces them. That is a principle that has already been written into the scope of our existence. It is a firm rule, just as undeniable and dependable as the law of gravity.

My Prayer: Father, touch those qualities that you placed in me and breathe life into them. The reply that I hear is, "OK!!"

Evil Desires

Scripture reading: James 4:1. *"What is causing the quarrels and fights among you? Isn't it because there is a whole army of evil desires within you?"*

James tells it like it is. He confronts people directly. When James hoes a row, he hoes it all the way to the end. James knows about the importance of purity in our innermost beings. He may have been slow to respond to the truth proclaimed by Jesus, but eventually he came to see the wisdom of what Jesus was saying. A friend, Mark Greenfield, writes, "It is cool when a light goes on in my head." James must have experienced a moment when a light went on in his head. It is experiences like these that keep us on a pilgrimage. Faith is the extension of the "Ah-has" in our lives. These "Ah-has!" eventually lead us to realize that there is a core to our beings and we can be "good at the core" or "rotten at the core". And all the behavior that flows from us will flow from our core. Even good behavior is tainted when our cores are rotten.

My Prayer: Father, can Jesus, residing within me, transform these evil desires seething within me? The reply: *"Absolutely! He can and He is!"*

Real Prayer

Scripture reading: James 4:3. *"And even when you do ask you don't get it, because your whole aim is wrong— you want only what will give you* pleasure."

Here is the reason our prayers go unanswered. (We don't like to admit this!) Real prayer comes from the deep within us (the desires of our hearts). With a tainted core, our prayers will be slanted toward self-interest. Our prayers will not be what God wants; they will be what we want. Even when our prayers are something that God wants, our prayers are still slanted by our inner being. We may deny the prayer that is on our lips by the prayer that resides deep inside us. Real prayer is when the desires within our hearts are the same as the desires deep within God's heart. Real prayer does not just want something; real prayer is the consistency between that which is upon our lips and that which resides within our innermost beings (hearts).

My Prayer: Father, am I onto something here? Could a fresh tamed core open a door to real prayer with real results? The reply that I hear is, **"Yes, to both questions."**

With Friends Like This—God Needs No Enemies

Scripture reading: James 4:4 (partial). *"...Don't you realize that making friends with God's enemies—the evil pleasures of this world— makes you an enemy of God."*

James does not say that making friends with God's enemies makes Him our enemy. He says it makes us an enemy to God. If we refuse to go forward to a pilgrimage into our inner life and the renewal of our innermost being, we are living precariously, for our relationship with God is estranged. Steeped in our Western culture, we are highly vulnerable here. Greek philosophy has mingled itself with our theology. We are bent toward Plato's concept of man as a trichotomy. We blend this philosophy into the gospel message and are prone to give our souls to God for safekeeping while retaining the remainder of ourselves for our purposes. This leads to partial commitments and partial journeys into godliness. Such a position leaves us with an impure inner life, and we cannot reap the rewards of wholeness or holiness. With friends like this, God needs no enemies.

James Gibson

My Prayer: Father, can anything be done to awaken our great Western culture to these realities? The reply I hear is, "Yes! You can make the pilgrimage within, find the flaws that beset you at the core, and present them to me for healing. My strategy is, ONE AT A TIME."

An Incomplete Journey

Scripture reading: James 4:4 (partial). *"...I say it again, that if your aim is to enjoy the evil pleasure of the unsaved world, you cannot also be a friend of God."*

Partial commitment will not lead us very far into a journey within. What can jump-start us into a serious spiritual pilgrimage? First, we can open the eyes of our heart to see the added suffering that our waywardness brings to Jesus who has already suffered enough. Second, we can draw near to those who are serious pilgrims and be inspired and awakened by the qualities in their lives. Finally, we can ask God to get us out of the rut traveled by so many in our culture and blast us into another orbit, traveling a road less traveled.

My Prayer: Father, am I listening to the right music? Do the drums that I hear beating, beat for me? Have you really summoned me to walk with you and live life like you would live it? The reply that I hear is, "Yes! Yes! Yes!" And I respond, "Can I do this without uncovering all the garbage that resides within me?" And I hear God replying, "No!"

The Pilgrimage Within

Scripture reading: James 4:9-10. *"Let there be tears for the wrong things you have done. Let there be sorrow and sincere grief. Let there be sadness instead of laughter, and gloom instead of joy. Then when you realize your worthlessness before the Lord, he will lift you up, encourage and help you."*

"Ah-ha!" Now we know why we cannot live life like God would live it without uncovering all the garbage that resides within us. Such a horrifying inner journey precipitates the repentance necessary for our new life. A mentor, Dr. Nat Tracy, would say, "If you can honestly look inside and not repent, then you are free not to repent." But, be assured that a journey within will uncover enough garbage to bring a flood of tears, sorrow, grief, sadness and gloom. So let it be!

My Prayer: Father, when I make the pilgrimage within and uncover the garbage there, intuitively, I know that I will be brought low. Will you be there to lift me up and encourage me? The reply that I hear is, **"James, you cannot imagine how high I will lift you up and the exuberance that will gush out of you!"** *And I respond, "So let it be!"*

Arrogance and Humility

Scripture reading: James 4:6.*"But he gives us more and more strength to stand against all such evil longings. As the Scripture says, God gives strength to the humble, but sets himself against the proud and haughty."*

Arrogance results when we resist the pilgrimage within, for without an inner pilgrimage, we will not realize the brokenness inhabiting our innermost beings. I resisted the pilgrimage within for a long time, fearing that my already poor self-esteem would be permanently destroyed by the onslaught of revelations hiding there. However, what I found there was a list of unresolved issues that were fermenting and poisoning my innermost being, leaving me with arrogance and without humility. It was the poison from those issues that was destroying my self-esteem. The only way that I could discover and deal with those issues was to venture within and look at them seriously. Yes, I have been brought low, but my self-esteem has not been destroyed. In fact, it has been elevated. And the false pride and air of superiority with which I surrounded myself have melted. The pilgrimage within has made me a better person with a stronger sense of self-worth. I recommend the journey to all who have a relationship with Jesus and a supporting community of caring people to hold them by the hand and support them as they venture within.

My Prayer: Father, thank you for Jesus and thank you for friends who helped me to make the frightening pilgrimage within. The reply that I hear is, "I am glad that you are taking the trip!"

Closeness With God

Scripture reading: James 4:8 (partial). *"And when you draw close to God, God will draw close to you."*

Who is the initiator? It is God. James may leave the impression with us that we are the initiators, but we are not. God comes to us first. This is the message in the incarnation. Now, James' scenario can begin to operate. When we respond to the initiation of God, we will be responded to by an additional move of God toward us. And what is it that God is looking for in the selection of His family? Is it a pure heart and clean hands? In a way, Yes! But this is something for which God can wait. First, God looks for a hungry heart; then He makes His move toward us, and we move closer to Him. It is our closeness with God that initiates the cleansing of our hearts and hands.

My Prayer: Father, thank you for seeking for me! I could never have responded, if you had not made the first move. Now, let's get on with the business of creating a pure heart and clean hands.

Lifting Others

Scripture reading: James 4:12 (partial). *"...So what right do you have to judge or criticize others?"*

A critical attitude is a good indication that we have not traveled far upon our pilgrimage within. The journey within takes all the puff and brag out of us. Those characteristics are replaced by another spirit. It is the spirit of acceptance, which embraces every human being as a brother or sister. If we keep the door to our inner life shut and locked, it is because we are afraid to see what resides there. Such fear about our being prompts us to pull others down so we will not look so bad in our own eyes. Do we want to be such persons? Of course not! As frightening and distasteful as it appears, we have no viable alternative but to venture within. Our reward is not only a cure for arrogance, but also we are rewarded with self-acceptance that allows us to give life instead of taking it.

My Prayer: Father, allow me to lift others. The reply that I hear is, **"Permission granted!"**

Soaring With Eagles

Scripture reading: James 4:14. *"How do you know what is going to happen tomorrow? For the length of your lives is as uncertain as the morning fog-now you see it, soon it is gone."*

In moments of deep reflection, I sense that greatness resides within me. Then that sense fades and another sense moves across the screen of my mind. It is a sense of brokenness and distortion. Which is the real me? Both! It is crucial that we enter into a pilgrimage that results in discovery of both our brokenness and our greatness where healing and awakening can occur. It is crucial that we begin now! There is one thing certain about life: Soon it will be gone! Discovery of ourselves requires diving into the blackest gorges of our lives. Debbie Parish, a friend, reminded me of a quote by Herman Melville.

> *"..And there is a Catskill eagle in some souls that can alike dive down into the blackest gorges, and soar out of them again and become invisible in the sunny spaces. And even if he for ever flies within the gorge, that gorge is in the mountains; so that even in his lowest*

> *swoop the mountain eagle is still higher than other birds upon the plain, even though they soar."*
> *Moby Dick, Herman Melville*

God rejoices in the carefully examined life. In God's eyes, when we moan as we dive into the darkest gorges of our lives, we are soaring with Catskill eagles. In God's eyes, when we revel as we become invisible in sunny spaces, we are likewise soaring with Catskill eagles. I can almost hear God shouting, "attaboy" or "attagirl".

My Prayer: Father, how am I doing? Sometimes I feel that I am soaring with eagles and at others, I feel that I am bogged down. The reply that I hear is, **"James, you face internal issues, and I am sure you feel that you will never overcome them; but you do and for a period you soar with eagles. Then you face the next issue and again, you feel bogged down. Progress is measured in terms of where you are soaring. Be content that you are upon a pilgrimage! I am!"**

Major Issues

Scripture reading: James 4:17. *"Remember, too, that knowing what is right to do and then not doing it is sin."*

It is easy to allow lesser issues to consume our time and energy (life). So, it is possible to drift through life without focusing either upon our selves or our major issues. Among those major issues are the questions: 1) Who am I? 2) What is my destiny? (Where am I going?) 3) Who is God and what is He like? Resolution of these questions requires a serious spiritual journey. We must not dillydally for if we do, we will come to the end of our lives with unresolved issues. James says, " Remember too that knowing what is right to do and then not doing it is sin."

My Prayer: Father, I would like to finish well. So, help me to focus upon the major issues—to enter into a serious spiritual journey and to find some fellow travelers to journey with me. The reply I hear is, **"I promise to be diligent in fulfilling your request!"**

The Dangers of Wealth

Scripture reading: James 5:1. *"Look here, you rich men, now is the time to cry and groan with anguished grief because of all the terrible troubles ahead of you."*

Material values without spiritual values will end in catastrophe for us. On a world scale, most Americans would qualify as rich people. Regrettably, many have deified the material and are on a journey toward terrible trouble. The proper handling of wealth is a far greater challenge to us, than the handling of poverty. Poverty can draw us into spiritual pursuits. Wealth usually does not. Wealth promotes an attitude of self-sufficiency in us and this becomes a barrier between our relationship to God and others. This places us in double jeopardy, for we may lose more than a relationship to God. We may lose a relationship to God and a relationship to the poor. In addition, we often have difficulty relating to others who are prosperous. Material values can lead us to a lonely existence. It is not that God does not love us; He loves us deeply and desires higher values for us. But, with mostly material values, we may never respond to God and our need for relationship with Him. Also, our many involvements, made affordable by wealth, rob our time and energy (life), and we are left without the opportunity for a close relationship with God, the poor, and other affluent people.

My Prayer: Father, by the world's standards, I am wealthy. How am I handling it? The reply, "Not as well as I would like, but you will survive it!

A Person or A Thing?

Scripture reading: James 5:3 (partial). *"...yet it (material values) will stand as evidence against you, and eat your flesh like fire..."*

We have been pre-constructed so that whatever we love (value) is assimilated into our being. If we love God, we will become like Him. If we love matter, we become like a thing. The values residing within us determine whether we become a person or a thing. Do we want to become a bundle of molecules or a person? The destinies of bundles of molecules cannot be very exciting. Bundles of molecules become zombies resembling persons, but they lack the exuberance of life that is enjoyed by persons. Therefore, we must be careful to find that which is of supreme value and pursue that. Failure to do so will have fatal consequences upon us. James says that material values will eat our flesh like fire.

My Prayer: Father, loving you is very important for me, isn't it? The reply, **"Why did you think that I wanted you to love me? It is not just for my sake; it is for yours as well!"**

Breaking The Spell

Scripture reading: James 5:5. *"You have spent your years here on earth having fun, satisfying your every whim, and now your fat hearts are ready for the slaughter."*

James is not very diplomatic. It is a little crude to compare people to feed lot cattle. But it fits the choices of many people. How can we break the spell of material values? Core values are imbedded deep within us. We cannot by an act of our will extract those values. We are wholly dependent upon something outside of us. If the character of God and the beauty of His being cannot get the attention of the deep within us, then we are goners. But, God assures us that He can solicit our attention. Discovery of those captivating aspects of God's character are made in a relationship with Him. That relationship begins when we invite Jesus into partnership with us. The sincere invitation that we give to Jesus to reside in us is responded to with His presence. That presence is working miracles of transformation within the deep of us that we could never have accomplished alone.

My Prayer: Father, I am so glad that you are changing me. I praise you for the love that prompted you to take an interest in a person like me. Thank you for choosing the kind of life that is greater than things. You have my permission to continue miracles of transformation within me. I hear God laughing and replying, "Thank you very much for giving to me what I already have. But, I am glad that you give me the permission to do what I already wanted to do. It is beneficial when both of us are traveling in the same direction."

The Lord's Return

Scripture reading: James 5:7 (partial). *"Now as for you dear brothers who are waiting for the Lord's return, be patient..."*

There are three ways that Jesus may be embodied in the world: 1) He can bodily return in what is known as the Second Coming. 2) His life may be embodied in us. 3) The continuing presence of His spirit in the world. If James is referring to the Second Coming, his admonition to be patient does not mean that we are to wait doing nothing. James has already made his case for patience as a virtue in those who are on a pilgrimage toward growth in godliness. It would be a mistake for us to wait for the Second Coming to begin our journey toward godliness. Jesus is the prototype for the new race of beings that God is raising up. As God's Son, He shares the same character that is in God. As followers of Jesus, we should be on our journeys toward becoming persons with much of that same character in us. We can be patient here also, but we should be progressing upon our pilgrimage toward growth in godliness. In no case should we allow patience to lull us into doing nothing.

My Prayer: Father, lure me and other Christians into an exciting pilgrimage toward your kind of life.

Is It Near?

Scripture reading: James 5:8. *"Yes, be patient. And take courage, for the coming of the Lord is near."*

The presence of Jesus in the world can be experienced in three ways. His return in the Second Coming, the continuing presence of His life and presence in the world, or by His presence in those who invite Him into their lives. The tarrying of the Second Coming of Jesus should not weary us. But the slowness of our journey toward godlikeness should! Could the coming of the Lord's kind of life in us be near? Let's hope so! But, Jesus deserves better vessels than we are providing Him. In whose court does the responsibility lie? Our regeneration is a joint effort between the Godhead and us. If it lies solely in our court, then is our salvation by self-effort? It cannot be! For if the responsibility lies solely within us, we will surely fail. The infusion of godlikeness into us is greatly in His hands, not ours. The slow progress that we are making may be necessary for the efficiency of the enterprise. If this is true, then we must be patient, waiting upon God to produce our growth in godliness in His own way and time. However, we can contribute to the process by making ourselves readily available, and even then we are dependent upon the winsomeness of God's being to draw us within His range.

My Prayer: Father, I would like for your kind of life to be infused into me. The response I hear is, "Are you sure you want this, for my kind of life has a price tag?" And I respond, "I think so! Help me to want it more!" And God responds, "Ok!"

Wrong Again

Scripture reading: James 5:9 (partial). *"Don't grumble about each other, brothers. Are you yourselves above criticism?"*

When the first inkling of understanding about what God is doing in the world descended upon me, my first response was to look at the church that had produced one so blind as myself and be critical of the church. If there is a way to mess up, I will find it. Verbally attacking and blaming the church for our weakness is getting it wrong again! Truth can be used in a way that alienates others who need to respond to it. We need to learn that the church is not the enemy. We also need to learn that moving toward a better understanding still leaves us with only partial understanding, for we are still among the broken who need better vision and additional healing. The best response for the rejuvenated Christian is to quietly enter into his or her journey toward exuberant life and allow the impact of that life to have its effect. Our criticism of the church may set back our own growth in godliness and the growth and development of others. We may need to ask for forgiveness because of our immaturity that has set back the growth and development of others and ourselves.

My Prayer: Father, forgive me for all those that my immaturity alienated and set back in their journeys. The reply, **"you have already been forgiven!"**

Suffering Is Our Friend

Scripture reading: James 5:11 (partial). *"We know how happy they (the prophets) are now because they stayed true to him then, even though they suffered greatly for it..."*

I cannot think of any strong Christians who have not been through suffering? It was the love of God for His children that prompted Him to refashion a world full of suffering. It was God's love for Adam and Eve that prompted Him to remove them from a comfortable place and put them in a difficult place after their fall. Suffering is the forge in which the metal of our character is hammered into stronger steel. Yet, it does not strengthen all. Why? The attitude that we take toward suffering is the pivotal point that determines what suffering does for us. A silversmith holds silver in the heat of his flame until all the impurities are burned out of it. He can tell when all the impurities have been burned out of the silver by looking for his own reflection in the liquid silver. We should be glad when suffering comes our way. However, we do not always receive it so freely. But, we can remain true to our faith that God is our friend and on our side. Such acceptance of suffering always ends in strengthening our godly character. My friend and mentor, Nat Tracy, would say, "It was the north winds that made the Vikings."

My Prayer: Father, suffering comes whether I view it properly or not. Somewhere along my journey, you taught me that suffering could be a friend. Thank You! The reply, **"Thank you for being open to this reality."**

Suffering, God's Tenderness and Mercy

Scripture reading: James 5:11 (partial). *"...Job is an example of a man who continued to trust the Lord in sorrow; from his experiences we can see how the Lord's plan finally ended in good, for he is full of tenderness and mercy."*

Some who have endured great sorrow have difficulty believing that a God of mercy would refashion the world so there would be suffering. Humanity's fall made a plan necessary. So, God came up with a test to determine whose kind of life is supreme. The kind of life that is supreme will endure. Suffering was the test to determine the kind of life that is supreme, and God saw suffering as a way for us to validate the quality of our lives. Even when sorrow determines that our kind of life is inadequate, we are blessed, for now we have the chance to discover the kind of life that is better. It is essential that we validate for ourselves the kind of life that prevails, and suffering can spur us toward this discovery.

Satan rejected God's kind of life and substituted his own quality of life as best. Satan's self-centered kind life will not handle suffering well. For, he and all those who follow in his steps will wallow in resentment of anything that robs them of comfort and self-satisfaction. Their self-pity will diminish them and cause them to shrink in stature.

We need to remember that the validation that is taking place here has consequences beyond this world. Angels are witnessing this demonstration and discovering that God's choice of love and servanthood is a valid choice, even though the love-servanthood kind life may lead to greater pain. Eventually, it can never, in all eternity, be questioned that God's kind of life is supreme.

My Prayer: Father, You really are full of tenderness and mercy and making a world where there is sorrow is another proof of it. The reply that I hear is, "James, you are blessed for you are seeing what few in the world see."

Privileged or Victimized

Scripture reading: James 5:11 (partial). *"....Job is an example of a man who continued to trust the Lord in sorrow; from his experiences we can see how the Lord's plan finally ended in good, for he is full of tenderness and mercy."*

Some feel victimized by God's decision to place them in a world that is like a hot furnace. We are not victims—we are privileged, for we have been offered the opportunity to partner with deity. We are created in God's image. The same kind of life that God prefers resides in us. If we choose His kind of life, then suffering helps us to internalize and awaken the character that God has already given to us. If we reject God's kind of life, then we make ourselves to be the victims of the sorrows and troubles of this world. In all fairness to God, we need to remember that God has chosen to place Himself in the furnace with us. And He has taken upon Himself a double portion of those sufferings that we are to partake in.

My Prayer: I praise you, Jesus, Father, and Holy Spirit! I praise you, Father, for your tenderness and mercy, and I do not feel victimized by the troubles and sorrows that beset me. I thank you for them and ask that you help me to take them and make something beautiful from them.

Props Are Not Necessary

Scripture reading: James 5:12 (partial). *"But most of all, dear brothers, do not swear either by heaven or earth or anything else; just say a simple yes or no..."*

Our insecurity and uncertainty form a base of weakness in us that prompts us to try to add strength to our words. When we see the truth, are the truth, do the truth, and say the truth we do not have to prop up our words with anything. An aroma rises from such persons. More than our words communicate honesty, sincerity, and conviction—our beings have a better way of doing this than words.

My Prayer: Father, help me to accept the truth that communication, which arises out of a proper being, does not need props. And I want to thank you for majoring upon my being instead of my doing. The reply that comes is, "James, it is you who majors upon minors, not me!"

Keep Praying

Scripture reading: James 5:13 (partial). *"Is anyone among you suffering?..."*

Absolutely! There are 3 of my friends battling with cancer. Another family is dealing with tragic, untimely death. Other friends are struggling with the infirmities of aging and approaching death. Some are in financial struggles. There are troubles in all shapes, sizes, and forms continuously filtering through my small circle of family and friends. James says, *"...He should keep on praying about it..."* Why? God placed us in a troubled world for some purpose, and that purpose is to be found in our prayer and meditation life. Prayer is not trying to squirm out of our problems; it is dialogue with God out of which a sense of understanding and purpose arises. God may not wave a magic wand and make the troubles go away, but He will bring us to a place of understanding, acceptance, and peace in the midst of suffering. Sometimes it is in our prayer and meditation that a solution comes to us. In addition, when we talk with God, we are also speaking to the God that is already residing within us. This summons the best that is within us to face and meet the crisis. In such a scenario, the best possible outcome is always realized.

My Prayer: Father, I pray that all my troubled family and friends will keep talking to you. Their prayers may not be perfectly right, but in the dialogue they will be drawn nearer to you and to the best possible resolution of their problems. The response I hear is, "I pray that they will too."

A Healthy Spirit

Scripture reading: James 5:13 (partial). *"...And those who have reason to be thankful should continually be singing praises to the Lord."*

The key phrase is, "reason to be thankful". If we focus upon the negative, then we will fail to direct our attention toward the positive. This is not healthy. Much of our trouble is unnecessary. We bring it upon ourselves by focusing upon negatives. If we focus upon illness, we will more likely become ill. If we focus upon good health, we usually are healthy. However, our focus is not an act of our will. Our focus arises out of animations that rise from deep within us. A healthy spirit is of great importance to good health. Upon discovery of non-treatable malignancy a person with a healthy spirit says, "I cannot believe that God would find me worthy of this!" The unhealthy spirit says, "I cannot believe that God would do this to me!" It is the first responder who sometimes amazes the medical community and survives.

My Prayer: Father, help me to stay positive. Create a spirit within me that has a healthy outlook upon life. I thank you for the progress that has already been made in me, and I praise you for the progress that I know will come.

Koinonia*

Scripture reading: James 5:14. *"Is anyone sick? He should call for the elders of the church and they should pray over him and pour a little oil upon him, calling on the Lord to heal him."*

The practice of spiritual healing has been negatively impacted by the abuse of some healing ministries. Misguided spiritual healers have used the act of spiritual healing as an attraction to themselves. Such displays are nauseating and create a distrust of healing ministry. It is beautiful when Christian brothers and sisters draw near to one another in a time of illness to offer their concern and support. When concern is genuine and not just a show of concern, there are powers released for which we have no explanation. Such healing incidents are not ritualistic. They are to be a coming together of a Christian family to support, encourage, and pray for the needy member. When the gathered body is a group that has participated in authentic *koinonia*, the place where they are gathered becomes electrified by a presence uncommon to anything else in the world.

My Prayer: Father, if there could be more koinonia in our churches, there would be less unnecessary illness and death. What can I do to encourage koinonia in

James Gibson

dry churches? The reply is, "Find someone in your church who is open to you, lower your own barriers of separation, and proceed toward the bonding of your spirits. If success is achieved, there will be others who want in on what the two of you have found. Then there will be others who...."

*Koinonia is a transliteration of a Greek word for which we have no English equivalent. We do not have words to express this level of intimacy, so the only way to understand it is to see it, then experience it. Even soldiers who train together and fight for their lives together are not bonded equivalent to this. This becomes not a closed society but an open society. Only those who keep their own barriers of separation in place will be excluded.

Healed Spirits

Scripture reading: James 5:15. *"And their prayer, if offered in faith, will heal him, for the Lord will make him well; and if his sickness was caused by some sin, the Lord will forgive him."*

If these promises are taken without the context of the descriptions made in the previous meditation, there may be confusion and disappointment. The bonded group of Christians armed with unity of spirit can accomplish together amazing accomplishments. The healing of bodies is small compared to the healing of spirits that can occur where there is *koinonia.* Those who find *koinonia* find a rich treasure, and wherever they go they will find *koinonia*, create *koinonia,* or be restless for the remainder of their lives. A key to renewing the strength of the church lies in the rediscovery and experience of *koinonia.* Lowering our barriers of separation and forming a bonded family is the key to stronger churches.

My Prayer: Father, my greatest failure in my ministry has been the failure to engender authentic koinonia. I wish that I could give myself to others and experience the giving back that produces an unbreakable bond of koinonia. The reply I hear is, **"James, you did well. It was not perfect, and you are forgiven; now go and try again. Your life is not over."**

Confession, Where God Can Be Touched

Scripture reading: James 5:16 (partial). *"Admit your faults to one another and pray for each other so that you may be healed...."*

One of the benefits of *koinonia* is the availability of kindred spirits to whom we can make confession. This is not mutual confession of sin without a supporting base. The bonding and supporting base is to be in place before heart-wrenching confessions are made. When barriers to bonding are lowered, kindred spirits are welded together, and there is integrity and reliability for the kind of intimacy that allows trust. Confessions made to such kindred spirits are like confessions made to God, and the God in my brother or sister is visible, touchable, and believably real. Prayers by other kindred spirits release powers seldom experienced in this world. In the hothouse described above confession ends in healing not frustration.

My Prayer: Father, give me kindred spirits for my healing. The reply, **"You have had them, and you will have others. Use them."**

Healing Our Past

Scripture reading: James 5:16 (again) and (partial). *"Admit your faults to one another and pray for each other so that you may be healed...."*

Confession empties poison from our spirit like vomiting empties a troubled stomach. I recall a personal confession experience: The bond was in place, and the supporting base of integrity was present. It had taken five years to build this unity and trust. I walked into his office and declared, "I need a garbage-can to throw up in." His reply was, "I would be delighted." I emptied every sinister element that I could dredge up. It was an awful two-hour exposure of spiritual brokenness. My confessor just listened. When I could find no other exposure of my sinful nature to relate, he asked, "Is that all?" It really wasn't, but at the moment I could not think of or dare to look at any more. I do not remember his exact words, but the context of his response was that I had been a rather puny sinner. For a moment I was sorry that I had not done a better job of it. We prayed together, and I walked out of his office as light as a feather. Where would I be today if it had not been for this person who for a moment fleshed God for me?

My Prayer: Father, it was your life in this person that enabled me to empty the garbage of my past. Thank you for Nat Tracy and other persons who have enabled me to be free of the past. The reply, **"James, you have been blessed. Now, be a blessing."**

Great Power

Scripture reading: James 5:16 (partial). *"...The earnest prayer of a righteous man has great power and wonderful results."*

We should never take this promise out of the context of the verses that precede it. It will be true only if the righteous man fits the preceding description. When the description fits, there will be incidents transcending Elijah's experience (James 5:17-18). Elijah prayed that it would not rain, and it did not for three-and-one-half years. Then Elijah prayed that it would rain, and it did. We have not touched the hem of the garment in this matter. We have missed so much.

My Prayer: Father, forgive me for having nuclear fission within my reach and using an air gun.

Wanderer Or Rescuer

Scripture reading: James 5:19.   *"Dear brothers, if anyone has slipped away from God and no longer trusts the Lord, and someone helps him understand* the *Truth again, that person who brings him back to God will have saved a wandering soul from death, bringing about the forgiveness of his many sins.*
Sincerely,
James"

Which player in the above scenario am I—the wanderer or the rescuer? My trust has not been what it should be, so I must be a wanderer. Yet, much truth has impacted my life and some acknowledge that my ministry has helped them, so I must be somewhat a rescuer. Who am I? I am the never to-be-duplicated masterpiece that God is recreating. God's creativity is still working with me fashioning expanding life in me that has no end. It is my hope that my journey will generate life in others. If it does, I will be bringing others back to God and bringing about the forgiveness of their sins.

Which player in James' above scenario are you—the wanderer or the rescuer? We who are the never to-be-duplicated masterpieces that God is recreating can and should be rescuers.

My Prayer: Father, thank you, thank you, and thank you! The reply I hear is, **"It delights me more than it does you."**

The Spirit of James

The spirit of Jesus' brother, James, has flowed down through the centuries and now rests upon us. I am truly grateful for the honor of sharing this journey with you. I will never be the same as I once was because of James. I hope that this will be true for all of you.

I am enclosing a quote from a fellow missionary's monthly report. It gave me hope, and I joyously cried!

> "If we could see as our Father sees, I am convinced we would be amazed at the size of His family. If the spiritual iceberg were suddenly turned upside down and exposed for all to view, the magnitude of the Church He is building would literally take our breath away."

> *I looked and there before me was a great multitude that no one could count, from every nation, tribe, people and language, standing before the throne.* (Revelation 7:9, NIV)

My Prayer: Father, may the spirit of James, Jesus' brother and your servant, flow down through the centuries and rest upon us. If it could be possible, may a double portion of James' spirit and power invade our beings and transform us into servants to our world.

God Bless,
James the Lesser

EPILOGUE

A friend, Cindy Chapman Wallace Jones, responded to one of my health updates with the following letter:

> When I read about Israel crying out in panic against Moses and God just days after leaving slavery in Egypt, I struggle to understand how *they* could not trust Him. He had just worked amazing miracles on *their* behalf to free *them* from Pharaoh. He made Himself literally visible to *them* every moment to help *them* believe.
>
> Then I find myself facing a new year when so many people I love are in a season of disease and fear about what lies ahead, and I begin to see how very simple my judgmental mind can be.
>
> The Israelites are but a picture of my loved ones and myself. *We* know The Living God, personally and up close, having walked through darkness and overwhelming light with Him. He has made Himself known to *us* in many ways. He has told *us* up front that He has overcome the world.

So why do *we* panic when *we* look out upon the Red Sea on one side and Pharaoh's army on the other? Why do *we* fall into depression the second *we* are thirsty or grow tired of manna?

The answer, I guess, is: We are sinners. We are made of dust.

But, Hallelujah, we are also children of the King. His Spirit lives within us to remind us all the time that we are both loved and blessed—not according to the world's measuring devices, but according to His abundance. Our suffering is only for a little while. Our joy is for eternity. The future we worry about is described as wondrously exceeding anything we can even imagine.

Prayer:
Lord, teach us to lean back all the way into your waiting arms. Remind us over and over who you are and who we are and all that you have done for us year after year. Give us wisdom to discern your way through each day's trials and compassion to walk hand-in-hand with those you have chosen to walk with us. Use today's suffering to make us more like your Son and bring glory to you. Overflow our hearts with Thanksgiving and Love and make us instruments of your peace. Amen.

This letter encouraged me greatly, for I knew that it came from one who knew what James has been talking about, for she has been there.

ABOUT THE AUTHOR

James Gibson was born and reared in central Texas. He completed undergraduate studies at Rice University in Houston, Texas in 1958, and completed theological studies at Southwestern Baptist Theological Seminary in Fort Worth, Texas in 1962. After graduating from seminary, he studied under Dr. Nat Tracy at Howard Payne University in Brownwood, Texas--auditing his undergraduate courses for several years. Dr. Tracy and James Gibson served together as co-chaplains at the State Juvenile Rehabilitation Center in Brownwood, Texas for five years.

James Gibson was pastor of three churches in central Texas before founding an experimental house church on Lake Brownwood in 1968. This made it necessary to become a bi-vocational minister. This church pioneered in providing outdoor worship services for visitors to Lake Brownwood. Church by the Lake focused upon spiritual formation and experimented with various spiritual growth techniques. He remained the spiritual leader for Church by the Lake for 26 years until his partial retirement in 1995.

James' bi-vocational ventures were varied in nature. He was involved in residential home building for 34 years.

Simultaneously, his wife, Pat and he constructed and operated a mini-storage business in Bangs, Texas for 20 years and have operated a service ministry to hunters in Colorado for 30 years. James led in the formation of a partnership to purchase and operate a small ranch in Southwest Colorado. Until just over one year ago, he served as managing partner for this venture.

Pat and James have been married for 54 years. They have a wonderful family—a daughter-in-law, two sons, and three grandchildren. In their partial retirement they served as International Service Corps missionaries for the International Mission Board of the Southern Baptist Convention. James led in the construction of a building for the Nampula Bible Institute in Mozambique. Pat assisted the strategy coordinator for Mozambique. Together, Pat and James hosted short-term American volunteers coming to Africa to engage in various volunteer mission projects.

Writing has been a longtime interest for James. James wrote and published his daily meditations via the Internet for 5 years. In addition to this book, he has another book published, "Cosmic Warriors—Partners in the Ultimate Triumph of God".

James sees himself as a work in progress with promises to keep and miles to go before he sleeps.